I0105862

# Oscar's True Friends

## DJ Stutz

illustrated by Nina Hvozdzeva

Oscar's True Friends

This is a work of fiction.

Text copyrighted by DJ Stutz ©2024

Illustrations copyrighted by A 2 Z Press LLC ©2023

Library of Congress Control Number: 2024927568

All rights reserved. No part of this book may be

reproduced, transmitted, or stored in an information retrieval

system in any form or by any means,

graphic, electronic, or mechanical without prior written

permission from the author.

Printed in the United States of America

A 2 Z Press LLC

PO Box 582

Deleon Springs, FL 32130

bestlittleonlinebookstore.com

sizemore3630@aol.com

440-241-3126

ISBN: 978-1-962101-16-5

# Dedication:

*To Amarah and Lachlan who
always remind me to
be happy every day .*

This book belongs to

_____

In the vibrant waters of the coral reef lived Oscar, the most beautiful fish you'd ever see. Some of his scales gleamed in the sunlight. Other scales were bright beautiful colors that matched the coral reef. His long, elegant tail swished gracefully as he navigated the ocean currents.

Life was good in the sunlight zone.  It was beautiful, there was lots to eat, and the water was clear and warm.

Some of the other fish gazed at Oscar with envy.
"I wish I had scales like Oscar" murmured one.
"Imagine having a tail as beautiful as his," whispered another.
Eager to be beautiful like Oscar, they swam up to
him with some unusual requests.

A fish named Sunny swam up first and asked, "Oscar, can I have some of your shiny scales? Everyone just sees right through me, and no one notices me. I want to sparkle just like you!"
Oscar looked puzzled, "Taking my scales would hurt. You can't have them." And he swam away.

Then Stormy came and asked, "Oscar, will you share some of your colorful scales with me? All of my scales are the color of sand and it would be so nice to have beautiful colors like you." Oscar sighed, "That's not possible. It would hurt a lot for me to pull out my scales." And he turned around and swam away.

Finally, Dash swam up to Oscar. "Your tail is so magnificent!" he said. "Can I have some of it?" Oscar was very surprised by this request, and he shook his head. "No!  Sharing my tail would be impossible. It helps me swim and change directions."

Word spread among the fish about Oscar's refusal to share. They began to avoid him and called him names like 'snobby' and 'mean.' They told everyone to leave Oscar alone and not play with him.

Now Oscar didn't know what to do. He was afraid of the other fish. He thought they might hurt him and try to take his scales and his tail. But he was lonely. He was so confused, sad and frightened. Certainly, there was someone who could help him.

He heard about a manta ray that was loved by everyone and is very wise. Oscar decided to go ask him for advice.

The manta ray lived far away and it took a while to find him, but finally Oscar heard he was living at the edge of a coral reef. So, he swam for hours and found him.

Oscar swam up slowly because he was a little
nervous and afraid. But Mr. Ray listened
thoughtfully to Oscar's story.
He took some time to think quietly
for a while. Oscar waited without speaking.
He wanted to let Mr. Ray think.

After a while, Mr. Ray cleared his throat. "It seems to me that you have three choices. You can do nothing and learn to be happy alone. You can share your scales and your tail. Now, that's going to hurt, and the other fish will be happy for a while, but they will never be your friends....

....Or you can help them to learn that they are talented and amazing just the way they are. Show them there are things they can do - things you can't do with your scales and your tail. Help them to be happy with their own scales and tales."

"How can I teach them about how amazing
they are?" Oscar asked.
"In addition to being very handsome, you are also
very smart," Mr. Ray said. "I believe you are smart
enough to figure this out." And he swam away.

While he was swimming home, Oscar thought and thought, and he came up with a plan.
At school, there was a race. Everyone knew Dash was going to win. She was the fastest fish at school, but Oscar decided to join the race anyway.

After the race. Oscar went to Dash and said, "Good job!
I could never win a race like that. My tail is too
big and slows me down. You are so lucky."

On another day everyone saw a boat flying above them.
A monster fish suddenly appeared and saw Oscar.
The monster fish followed Oscar and tried
to catch him in a little net.

Oscar swam away as fast as he could. He was so afraid.
He hid deep in the coral until the big fish went away.
The monster fish didn't even see Sunny.

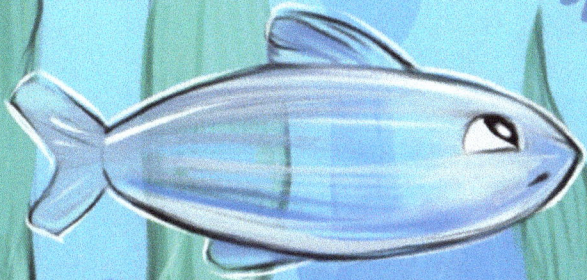

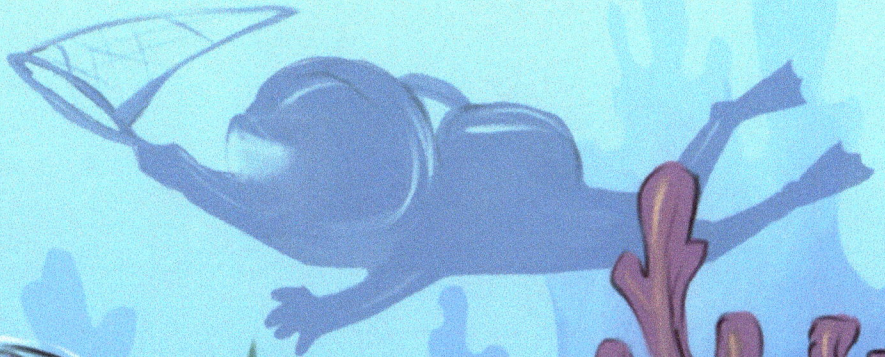

When the monster fish left, Oscar talked to Sunny. "You got to swim around free the whole time. You were safe. You don't have shiny scales and the big fish didn't want to catch you. You didn't have to be scared like me."

Finally, a dolphin came swimming in the coral reef. She saw the beautiful colors in Oscar's scales and thought he might make a tasty treat. Poor Oscar swam in among some other fish, but he was too easy to see. The dolphin kept chasing him. Oscar was so scared.

Quick! Hide behind me." Stormy said. "She will never see you."

Oscar thankfully swam behind Stormy and hid.
Stormy blew up big and round.
Surprised, the dolphin swam away.

"Thank you for letting me hide behind you. You saved my life. I am so easy to see with all of the colors in my scales. When you puffed up so big, you scared that dolphin away. You are so much safer than I am."

Later, the fish were together talking. Dash said, "I am so glad I don't have a tail like Oscar. He loses all the races."

Sunny said, "I am so glad I don't have shiny scales like Oscar. The big fish didn't try to catch me, but it really wanted to catch him."

Stormy said, "I am so glad I don't have colorful scales. That dolphin could see Oscar everywhere until he hid behind me. I scared the dolphin away because I can puff out. I am much safer."

The fish all agreed. Maybe being so shiny, colorful, and flowing isn't the best thing. It seemed that Oscar had a hard time with some things. "We are all so lucky to be who we are." They all agreed. "Maybe we should watch out for him. He needs our help."

Now all of the fish play together, and Oscar doesn't feel so lonely. Dash is fast, Sunny is invisible, and Stormy can blow up big and scare away dangerous fish, and Oscar has some good friends.

The fish have learned that it is okay to be exactly who you are and that they don't all have to be the same to be friends. In fact, being friends with fish who are different makes life a little better and a whole lot safer.

# The
# End

DJ Stutz is an Early Childhood Specialist and understands the importance of vocabulary for a child's success in academics, as well as emotional regulation and developing friendships. She is Mom to 5, Neina to 13 and Auntie to 70. Now, she lives on a farm on a prairie not far from Old Faithful where she coaches parents of young children and works on her podcast, Imperfect Heroes: Insights into Parenting.

# A Note from the Author

I hope you and your family enjoyed *Oscar's True Friends*! The story of Oscar and his colorful scales is more than just a tale about fish—it's a reminder of the beauty in celebrating what makes each of us unique.

You may have noticed that there's a growing push, in the name of equity, for everyone to be the same or have the same things. In our material world, children often feel pressured to want something just because a friend, classmate, or family member has it. It's also natural for kids to feel jealous if someone seems better looking, more athletic, or smarter than they are. While these feelings are normal, they aren't helpful to a child's social, emotional, or moral development.

That's why it's so important to guide our children in recognizing their own special abilities, cheering on the successes of others, and understanding that if they want to improve at something, they have the power to practice and grow. The same goes for material items—helping kids work and earn the things they desire teaches them responsibility, gratitude, and the value of hard work.

The following pages are filled with ideas and activities to help your child discover their unique gifts, celebrate the differences in others, and avoid the trap of jealousy or resentment. Together, we can raise children who see the beauty in diversity and understand that our world thrives because of—not despite—our differences.

By teaching your child to celebrate their own gifts and appreciate the differences in others, you're helping them grow into kind, confident, and compassionate individuals. Remember, we don't all have to be the same—thank goodness! It's the mix of talents, interests, and personalities that make families, communities, and our whole world work.

So go ahead—embrace the quirks, cheer for the effort, and celebrate the differences. After all, life would be pretty dull without them!


Let's dive in!

## Helping Your Child Shine

Every child is amazing in their own way, and as parents, we get to help them discover what makes them special! The truth is, no one has to be good at everything, and that's okay—our differences are what make the world such a colorful and exciting place. Imagine if everyone had the same talents or interests—boring, right?

Here's how you can help your child celebrate their unique gifts:

- **Let Them Explore:** Whether it's painting, building, dancing, or solving puzzles, give your child the chance to try new things. They might surprise you (and themselves!) with what they love.

- **Cheer for the Effort:** Instead of focusing on being the "best," celebrate their hard work. Try saying, "Wow, I love how hard you worked on that puzzle!"

- **Point Out Their Strengths:** Kids often don't realize how awesome they are until someone tells them. Say things like, "You're so good at making people laugh" or "I love how you take care of your little brother."

**Celebrate Being Different:** Remind your child that the world needs all kinds of people—artists, scientists, builders, teachers, and dreamers. Their unique talents are their gift to the world!

## Teaching Kids to Appreciate Differences

It's natural for kids to notice when others are different from them, but we can help them see those differences as something to celebrate instead of feeling jealous or left out. Here's how:

- **Talk About It:** Say things like, "Isn't it cool how Mia is so fast? And you're so great at drawing—imagine what a team you two would make!"

- **Read Together:** Find books about kids with different abilities, backgrounds, or experiences. Stories are a great way to show that everyone has something special to offer.

- **Focus on Teamwork:** Encourage activities where everyone's skills matter, like baking cookies or building a fort. Highlight how each person's contribution makes the project better.

**Let Them Help:** Look for opportunities where your child/ren can help you with something they are good at or want to learn more about. Invite them with terms like, "Hey Joey. You are so good at this. I could use your help."

# Fun Activities to Celebrate Differences

Here are some fun ways to help your child appreciate what makes them—and everyone else—unique:

## 1. Superpower Collage

Grab some paper, markers, and magazines. Have your child create a "superpower collage" filled with pictures or drawings of things they're great at. Then, make one for yourself, too! Share and celebrate each other's superpowers.

## 2. Family Talent Show

Host a family talent show where everyone can show off something they love to do—singing, dancing, storytelling, or even doing silly impressions. The rule? Everyone's talent is equally awesome!

## 3. The Differences Game

List things that make each family member unique, like favorite foods, hobbies, or talents. Then talk about how those differences make your family stronger. For example, "Mom loves to cook, Dad's great at fixing things, and you're the best at making us laugh!"

## 4. Compliment Jar

Set up a jar where family members can drop notes about what they love or admire about each other. Read the notes together once a week—it's guaranteed to bring smiles!

## 5. Big World, Many Gifts

Take a moment to imagine the world without differences. No bakers, no musicians, no doctors, no inventors. Help your child see that everyone's unique skills are what keep our world spinning.

## 6. Role Play Empathy

Pretend to "walk in someone else's shoes." Ask your child, "What do you think it's like to be the new kid at school?" or "How would it feel if you weren't picked to play on a team?" This helps them understand that everyone faces challenges—and it's okay to lend a helping hand.

www.ingramcontent.com/pod-product-compliance
Lightning Source LLC
Chambersburg PA
CBHW042333030426

42335CB00027B/3328